FROM DOPE FIEND 2 SON OF A KING

Bryon L. Johnson

TABLE OF CONTENTS

"But as many as received him, to them gave he power to become the sons of God, even to them that believe on his name"
(John 1:12).

CHAPTER 1

BORN IN SIN

September 30, 1973 was the date I made my entry into this world. I was born to William S. Lucas and Katrina Johnson in Grandy Park projects located in Norfolk, Virginia.

I came two years after my dad got out of the military in which he developed a heroin habit as a scared young man. My parents never married. In fact, I can't even remember them living together although my dad said we all did.

Sam, my dad told me of how he and my mom Tina met and started dating. According to him, he got into a fight with some guy name July. During the fight, his tongue got cut or bitten really bad. Mom started coming over to help take care of him considering he could only eat soup because of his tongue. Well, even as I write this, I can't help but to notice how much violence was there at the very beginning. As a matter of fact, it was violence that brought them together. I guess it's fair to say that I was "Born in Sin."

CHAPTER 2

SHAPED IN INIQUITY

My earliest memories start when I was about seven years old. I have heard that people can remember when they were two and three years old but I'm unable to do that due to extensive and continuous times of getting high. Back to my story, when I was about seven years old I remember the guy banging on our door really hard trying to fight another guy who was inside our house. You see my house was the bootlegger house. My mom sold liquor, beer and food to the local drinkers and partiers. I remember being really nervous and scared on this night. I was upstairs looking out of my window and I saw my dad come up to the guy who was yelling outside my house. After a short argument, my dad cut his throat. A few words were spoken and my dad came upstairs and said, "I saw you in the window." He then said, "You know I did that because of you. I had to protect you guys by stopping him from coming inside and hurting someone." On the next day, I remember looking around for a man who had a cut on his neck. I had an idea what house the guy stayed in on my same row but there were many guys who stayed there. I thought I could identify him by bandages on his neck. I knew that he didn't die because like always, I had eavesdropped on the adults' conversation.

Speaking of bootleggers and serving drunkards, I clearly remember one night I was sitting at the table doing my homework and there was a couple buying drinks while helping me with my homework. Shortly after, I found out they were the police doing an undercover sting operation. Needless to say, my mom caught herself a charge that night and I had to go the neighbors until she was bonded out.

When I was young, my mother was a pretty dark-skinned lady that wore glasses and had a coke bottle shape. The problem was that she didn't love herself. So, her life consisted of a continuous flow of boyfriends moving in and out of our house. Many of them were friends and most of them seemed not to like me much. What's amazing about the memory is that I can remember all of them. Most of them died prematurely. In those times most of her boyfriend's drunk *syrup*. It was the syrup that's in the brown bottle that makes you nod uncontrollably. These guys were bums and were just using her for sex and a place to stay. These guys were afraid of my dad because he was known for stabbing and shooting people. However, he stayed locked up most of the time. I guess they all thought it was a good idea to talk trash and to hit on me. The majority of these guys were verbal and physically abusive to my mom. Over the years, I've seen my mom take many beatings and I would often jump in. I was totally outmatched by these men. At a very young age, my nerves were shot and it manifested in my stomach regularly. Many nights I sat up and cried with momma. Usually, she was hurt because they left—and I was happy that they left. I remember saying, "Momma don't worry about him, all we need is us, momma." I would say, "Momma don't let him back in because he hurt you," but momma was lonely and always felt she needed a MAN. Momma wanted a man so much that she would even put me out the house to please them. At those times, I would walk to my grandma Margaret's house who lived in the same projects not too far away.

At momma Margaret's house, I ate breakfast, lunch, and dinner—something I wasn't used to at home. At grandma's house, we went to church and she taught us about Jesus. Grandma's house had a heap of cousins to play with. The one thing that I noticed most at grandma's house is that I felt loved. Grandma had a way of making everyone feel like they were the special one. I remember one day grandma asked me if I would like to live with her and I immediately said, "Yes." Somehow my mom found out and asked me about it while crying. She said they were trying to take me away from her. I remember her crying and saying how much she loved me and needed me. She then told me that if I loved her that I would stay with her. In other words, she made me feel horrible forever because I was considering leaving. However, I knew from a very young age that she loved partying and men more than she ever love me.

Well, one thing is for sure I vowed that as soon as I got a little bit older, her boyfriends wouldn't talk trash and get in my face anymore or else they would surely pay. I must tell you I kept to my word wholeheartedly. By the age of 13, I bought my first gun and immediately I gained much confidence. During that young age, I was selling drugs, stealing cars, and getting high.

My court was where all the money was being made in our projects. A lot of problems and murders that no young man should witness came with that money. Being without a father, I looked to the older hustlers for guidance. This is where my life took a major turn with robbing, using heroin, coke and chasing young girls. I wanted to be like them so much because they made it look good and so rewarding. I just couldn't resist. The new clothes, cars, and jewelry baited me in like animals in route to a trap. I never thought I would use heroin but they told me about how long you could have sex. My vulnerability concerning my inability to last long while having sex caused me to indulge. Needless to say, a dope fiend was born. Love at first sniff. My father was a dope fiend so immediately I knew I woke up a sleeping giant that came through my bloodline. From that point on I started to figure out ways to try to get away. During one of my court appearances for stolen cars I asked the judge if I could be sentenced to Job Corps and he agreed.

While in Flatwoods Job Corps, every time I would call home my momma told me she needs me home and made me feel guilty for being away as if I was her man. Not to mention, I had a girlfriend back in Norfolk who I thought of often although I knew it was *out of sight, out of mind* for her. Eventually, I left Job Corps and headed back to Grandy Park.

I stayed with mom a few months and I decided to go to live with my uncle in Woodbridge, VA. My intent was to go back to school and to do things right. However, soon after I arrived there my uncle was busted for selling drugs and the funny thing about that is nobody knew he sold drugs, at least I didn't. With my uncle locked up, and me being in a place where I didn't know anyone, I went back home and got my homeboy "O." We headed back to Woodbridge with coke and a plan to get money. I think it's worth mentioning that the entire time I was in Woodbridge, whenever I talked to my mom she made me feel bad about not being home by telling me how much she needed me. Whether I was attempting to do good or bad, when I was away, she always asked me to come back to that war zone.

Well, I came back home at age seventeen and my mom introduce me to a neighbor who was 24 years old. The next thing you know she's pregnant with her fifth child—thanks mom. Now at this time my heart has grown cold and I had allowed negative experiences to shape me. Because of the frequent changes of men by my mom, my perspective of women was twisted and I had lost respect for them. I allowed the men in my momma's life to cause my heart to change into one of stone and at any sign of disagreement, I was ready for war. In jail, I would say, "I'm trained to go." I'm a young ticking time bomb with no love and no respect for authority. This was brought on by the repeated abuse caused by people who should've protected me but instead they exposed me to the enemy.

CHAPTER 3

ME AND POPS

My earliest memories of Sammy Lucas, my daddy, consist of visiting him in prisons. In those times, Tina Childs was his girlfriend. Dad also had a child by Tina who went by the name of Marcus. Tina Childs was very nice to me and for years would come get me on weekends so that we could take a long ride to whatever prison Dad was in at that time. I remember taking food and drinks to the prison to eat while we visited Sam. Tina seemed to enjoy her visit with Sam but I think that she enjoyed Marcus and I bonding together more. Marcus was an only child needless to say he was spoiled beyond measure. During those times, he had every toy you could imagine. I can't help but to remember that his ears were incredibly big. Through the years his body eventually caught up with them.

After these brief memories of Sam in my adolescent years, the next thing I remember is him being released when I was at the life-changing age of seventeen. It was at that age when I encountered the Lord for myself. It was on the block where I met Jesus. I had been laying low because my friend had pulled out a gun on the biggest drug dealer in our neighborhood. The problem was, it was my gun and the dealer knew it belonged to me and not to mention the fact that I was present when it happened. This dealer responded by having his workers along with his cousin from New York to look for us. Immediately after the incident, I dropped my friend off out of Brambleton and I returned to the park to my house and stayed in for a couple of weeks. I heard that the New York boy was looking for us and that he was walking around with what appeared to be a machine gun or something. Finally, I got tired of hiding and came out and plus these were my projects. Anyways, I was born and raised in Grandy Park. So, the day that I got tired of hiding, I started walking through the circle in the front of the park. It was there that a minister by the name of Gregory Perry approached me about my eternal standing. On the spot, I began to weep and accepted Jesus Christ as my Lord and Savior. In an instant I stopped getting high, drinking, hustling and smoking cigarettes. God had delivered me in a dramatic way.

Although God had delivered me from many things I continued to *shack* and fornicate. Whenever you give the devil an inch, he will take a mile. I gave him a foothold and eventually it turned into a stronghold, which in turn kept me in a chokehold. Gregory Perry had given me job for a cleaning service at the shipyard. I had a group of brothers who were fresh in this new walk, just as I was. We all fellowshipped, hung out, and worked together. We shared our experiences as we grew together and encouraged one another. While on that job at the shipyard, I met a guy named Jack. Jack was a born again believer who was on fire for God and happened to have one arm. Everywhere Jack went and whomever he encountered, he would always tell people about the love of God. I never saw a time where Jack was discouraged or lacked faith. One day Jack asked me if I had been baptized in the Holy Ghost or filled with the Spirit with the evidence of speaking in tongues. I had no idea what Jack was talking about but if it was God, I wanted it. Needless to say, Jack prayed with me to be filled with the precious Holy Ghost with the evidence of speaking in tongues. God did exactly that. Speaking in tongues was kind of weird for me but I truly sense the presence of the Holy Spirit every time it happens with the results of feeling empowered and stronger in faith. It was during this period that my Dad was released from prison. When my Dad first got out, he was attending church and speaking about God also. I don't know how long it was but shortly after his release he decided that he wanted to get high and I went right along with him. I probably had been clean about 6 months and he had been clean some time since he was fresh out of the pin I'm assuming. Pops had a lot of pull on the streets so he could pretty much get what he wanted from anyone. On this day, we got about five or six bags free from this New York kid name Knowledge. We were creeping and sneaking in the back of Zo's house. We went upstairs and he started getting his works and paraphernalia together so he could shoot his dope while I sniffed mine. I snorted mine like a pro and went to the bathroom to put some water in my nose so I could *catch a drain*. Two minutes after I got back my Pops went out. That's right, first shot and he overdosed. I panicked and didn't know what to do. I yelled downstairs to Zo and said that something was wrong with Sam and from downstairs she yelled up, "Bryon, don't tell me that he was getting high," in which I responded, "He wasn't getting high." However, it was obvious that he was getting high because I didn't clean up. He still had the needle out, bags out, spoon out, and he was out. Zo went straight into medic mode and you could clearly tell that she done this a time or two before. Sam chest was swelling pretty big and it wasn't looking good. I call the paramedics and Zo worked on him until they came. Needless to say, that the entire neighborhood was outside as they wheeled him into the vehicle. I guess it's true what they say, "What's done in the dark will come to the light." After that near-death experience, we never went back to church. For me I think the shame kept me from repenting and going back to the house of the Lord.

We were both off to the races, chasing dope, and hustling. Next thing you know we were robbing together. I remember the first robbery clearly: I was in the back of the park and Sam pulled the gun on a dude who was trying to score. After he pulled the gun out, I punched the guy in the face and knocked him down. My reason was that I didn't want Sam to shoot him, he was known for that. Then after we got him to a safe place, Sam said, "Yea Bre, you did a good job." It was at

13

that very moment for the first time in my life that I could remember that my pops publicly acknowledged that he was proud of me. On that day, I took a mental note as to what I had to do to get my father to affirm me. I pursued that *street cred* and acknowledgement from Sam fervently from that day forth.

It wasn't too long before we went from robbing together to him robbing me. I guess there's no honor among thieves. We were right next door to my house 2937 Kimball Terrace and evidently, I ended up being the only one with dope and I didn't get the memo. For some reason, everybody and their momma was in the court that day. Sam, asked for some dope and I said I couldn't afford it because I had to get money to pay rent. At that time, I had an apartment out the Heights by the grill with my girlfriend, my son, and the rest of her kids. I told Sam I didn't have it and the next thing you know I was staring down the back of his gun while he was saying, "Bre, I'll kill you." On this day, I learned to love no one because even your biological father will get you. I think I was even more hurt from the fact that he did this in front of everyone. It sent a clear message and made me look pretty worthless. I remember making up my mind that I was going to kill him besides, I had two guns in my car. First, I went in the house and told my mom and while telling her I cried like a baby from the pain of being betrayed which would take years to totally get over.

I had been in jail for about six months and my dad walked

through the gates on the fifth floor. Immediately, I saw him and went over to holla at him. Without thought, I gave him my bunk and I slept on the floor do to the overcrowding of the jail. I must say that it was weird being locked up with my father when I had no memories of sharing a house together. Now we were sharing a cell together. As crazy as it seems, I was excited about spending time with him while doing my jail time. We started playing chess and he began to get dope sick as all heroin addicts do. Later that evening the nurse came around and she slipped him something. As soon as he took whatever it was that she gave him, he started tripping out. Pops was seeing things, looking into space, and talking like a little kid. He couldn't even talk or walk on his own. We yelled for the deputy and carried him to the gate where they took over to take him to the medical floor.

The next time I saw him was months later. I was in the Christian block and he was just walking by. We engaged briefly before he had to go. It was only a matter of time before DOC would come to get me considering I was sentenced to seven and a half years.

CHAPTER 4

CAUGHT A CASE

It was August 4, 1993 at 6:30pm when I caught my first case on 2900 block of Kimball Terrace in Grandy Park in the court where it all went down. This was the spot where all the hustlers, boosters, pimps, gamblers, prostitutes, and plucks would hangout or meet up.

It was early in the morning because I had a motto, "The early bird gets the worm." I was out there early, trying to make a dollar and little did I know that the bicycle police were heavy and active on that morning. I guess "The early bird gets the worm" was their motto also. I was in the court waiting on folks to come through to score. A few had come and it seemed like it was going to be a good day. All of a sudden, the bikes rolled up on me from everywhere. I took flight straight through the court. As I approached the end of the court, I jumped the fence while at the same time tossing a bundle of dope into a car that had people sitting in it. I was in hopes of them pulling with the diesel.

Evidently, they didn't pull off because when the police

finally caught me they had that dope also. I continue running across the street through Kimball Court. I hopped the fence by Mrs. Rose house. Mrs. Rose was the candy lady. I knew her kids, grandkids, and her big dogs. After I jumped the fence, I was now in the maze. I was very familiar with the maze because that's where my Grandma Margaret lived. I ran into a house that use to be Anna's. Everyone knew Anna and her kids KitaBoo, Fat's, and Tomeka. She no longer lived there and here I was, running up into someone's house I didn't know. I told the people I would pay them, then I ran upstairs to hide.

Honestly, I totally forgot I had crack in my pocket so I didn't even attempt to flush it. The police kept yelling from downstairs to come out with my hands up and come downstairs. Needless to say, I never did. If they were going to catch me they would have to come and get me which they did. The officers brought me downstairs, took me out on the back porch and began to search me while proceeding to put handcuffs on me. Everyone seemed to be outside but I remember Ms. Ida Mae clearly.

Ms. Ida Mae was my mother's friend and her son Face was my best friend. She was yelling at the police to make sure they didn't rough me up too bad. Even during those times, the police had a tendency to rough us young guys up from time to time. The officers talked to the squad car and took me to the P.O.C. on Virginia Beach Blvd. While at the station they did their usual good cop, bad cop routine.

They do this in hopes that someone will snitch but they quickly found out they had the wrong one as far as that's concerned. While at the police station, I was mad at myself, however at the same time I was proud because I had money in my safe to bond out.

I got to the jail in the booking area and I see Reggie so I said, "What up?" to him. Reggie grew up in our neighborhood but chose the right path. He was a deputy in the jail who worked in booking. It was in booking where I began to feel dope sick. I made a call to my mom from there. I now had the great task of getting my safe from Yvette's house to my mom's house where the key to the safe was. After a few calls, I just about gave up because my stomach was hurting. I was spitting up the lining of my stomach, my back was hurting, and everything I smelled stunk really bad. I was lying on the floor under the phone because the cell block was overcrowded. Sweating and irritated I noticed that all the fellas from around the way were in that block. I remember seeing Phil, Ralph, Pee-Wee, and Skipper from around the way. Ralph offered me chocolate and stuff to try to ease the kicking process.

I'm not sure if the chocolate did anything at all. Next thing I heard was Bryon Johnson, B&B. B&B was a term the deputies used to let you know you were leaving. It stands for Bag & Bags. It was sweetest sound you could ever hear. On the following date, September 1993 approximately around the same date I got busted again. You know the location—Kimball Terrace in the projects of Grandy Park.

This time the charges were reversed. I was charged with Distribution of Heroin and Possession of Cocaine. I was so high I didn't even try to get rid of the crack because I forgot all about it. I was back in the jail going through the same withdrawals and affects. However, this time there's no money in the safe. In fact, I didn't have much money at all. since I got out on bond I had been getting high more than ever. I probably contributed it to the pressure of the case, but the fact of the matter was that I was a dope fiend. So, with the money to post another $10,000 bond I had to get my mom to get in contact with my dad. That was going to be a task because my dad and most of all the hustlers in my neighborhood were in Texas to see the Sweet Pea Whitaker fight. It was about a week before my Dad sent a bondsman to get me out.

Once again, I was called for B&B. I went downstairs and the bondsman told me "Your dad said for me to give you a ride home." I was thinking to myself, "This won't look good at all. A white man giving me a ride to the hood after I just got busted," so I got him to drop me off in Chesterfield Heights so I could walk to the park. As soon as I got to the park, I saw Derick in the back of the court. I asked him to hook me up, he did and I was off to the races again.

I had Danny Shipley on both cases. At that time, he was an up and coming lawyer. He carried some weight on the streets for dope cases. On my first charge, I was sentenced to two years, with two years suspended, and two years' probation. On my second case I received five years with, five years suspended, and five years on probation. On both cases I took a plea deal.

By January 5, 1994, I was placed officially on probation after the plea deals from November 19, 1993. By March of 1994, I was back in jail for armed robbery and possession of a firearm by a convicted felon.

After this time, my addiction totally had the best of me and I was going down fast. I thought I could stick-up a young drug dealer and get away but in this case the streets were talking. Eventually, I pleaded guilty to larceny and received five years with all suspended but six months.

Needless to say, this violated me on my previous cases, so they gave me all my time from both cases. I ended up with seven years and six months to serve in the State Penitentiary. Here I was, it seemed like destiny fulfilled. Momma always told me I would be like my daddy. The neighborhood expected this of me. Some even prophesied it and spoke death over my life. Most of my friends were in there just getting out or on their way.

At the time I entered the jail, it was filled with drugs. Anything you wanted was there. Guys walking around high as gas. This was eye-opening to me. First bid I hadn't left the jail yet and I saw a young dude get turned out. I made up in my mind a long time before that I would never be my testimony and walk in that truth today.

In the beginning, I partook in getting high, gambling and fighting. As a matter of fact, I got my lip busted in the jail and had to go to the community hospital for stitches. It wasn't all bad though because I filled out a request to get into the Christian Block that was pretty new. I believe God drew me to this decision because most guys at the time chose not to go because of reputation but I felt a power that was drawing me and I didn't want to resist.

Once I began to engage in the lessons, activities, groups, and prayers, I knew that this was where I belonged. It was in this place that I really discovered God for myself and no longer worshipped the God of my grandmother. Almost immediately, I began to dream and have visions from God. I prayed fervently day and night and I enjoyed it. I lived by discussing the Scriptures and listening to tapes concerning the Gospel. When I read the Bible, I would escape jail for the moment and would find myself inside the stories of the Bible as an onlooker. In these dreams or visions, I could smell, taste, feel, and behold all it offered. For the first time in my life, I had peace even in the midst of a storm. This was the place I had been searching for in my spirit. I never imagined I would find it behind bars. For the first time in my life, I felt satisfied and loved.

When I began to realize that my 6 months were up and I was about to complete the program anxiety overtook me. I knew I had to go back to the cell block where survival was the only thing on my mind. It was place where every minute of the day someone was trying to get over on you.

After I entered back into regular population my fire was quickly burnt out. I found it true that bad communication corrupts good behavior. The darkness that once oppressed me was back and perhaps even stronger. Every man in there was pronouncing death over themselves and others. Poison from their tongues rolled off at a rapid rate.

Before you knew it, I was back gambling, cussing, and fighting stronger than before. I believed that the demon came back with seven more even stronger then him. My latter was worse than my former.

It wasn't much longer before I heard, "B&B." It was the day that I would take that ride to prison. My destination was Indian Creek receiving or intake. On this day, about six of us arrived to be processed. There was one Chinese guy, a man from Newport whose parents own stores. Everybody from the park was on this spread. Champ was in receiving with me. This would come in handy later on. At some point in my time, some guys thought I stole something and while I was on the toilet they tried to rush me but Champ came in the restroom in a nick of time. He must have known what was going on because I had no clue. My man Frashon was there. We were close and had gone to school together all the way until we got put out of middle school for fighting.

At Indian Creek, there were plenty drugs so needless to say, "I was back getting high." After about six months there, I was told to pack my bags I was being shipped to another prison. After boarding the bus, we took this long ride in the wee hours of the morning. When I looked up, we were at Powtan where there were many buses with hundreds of inmates on them shackled hand and foot. This is where we all got off and changed buses to whatever location we were going. For some reason, this reminded me of slaves being transported. I changed buses and took another long ride until I reached Camp 4 Baskerville, VA.

Once on Camp 4, I realized I knew a lot of guys on this camp. I was greeted by my cousin Tyrone, Vic, Lil Pat, Barry, Shawn, Ghost and Me-Me from the park.

I didn't like this prison because of the clay-like dirt that made everything white look dingy. Neither did I like the fact that I was put on the road gang. The Road Gang was the guys who bush axed and used the swing blade to chop down what seemed to be endless forest alongside the highway. Usually there were two guards with guns watching over us as we worked so that we wouldn't try to escape. I hated this because most of the time I was there it was freezing cold. We were out there working for 24 cents an hour. It was on this camp where I made work release during my annual review. Upon receiving this information, I chose to keep it to myself because I didn't need anyone trying to run my time up.

However, instead of sending me to a work release camp they sent me to James River— a work camp. Immediately, I went to the counselor to see why I was there. Needless to say, I had to stay there until a room came open at the work release camp. On this camp, protocol was at 6 AM in the morning we had to go outside and stand on the basketball court to get chosen to go out and work in freezing temperatures. I can't remember where I went or what I did because I only went out about two times before I decided to buck the system because I can't do cold. I was willing to lose it all because it was just too cold for me to work. I know some guys worked at Goochland the Women's Prison down the road however they put me in the field.

Amazing, I didn't get in trouble or get my work release revoked because I only stayed there about 3 weeks before I got shipped to Chesterfield, VA where the work release was.

On the unit, there were also a lot of guys I had encountered throughout the system. Here you had to stay in for a week or two before you went to work in the real world. In this time, you would get your social security card, birth certificate and etc.

After my two weeks, I went on an interview at Howard Johnson Hotel and got hired for a room-cleaning position. It had been over two years since I had been outside, so you can imagine everything that was going on in my mind. For some reason, I loved this period in my life, maybe it was because it was the first time ever that I was clean and working. With that being said, when it was time for me to get out, I was really scared and wouldn't have mind staying there.

At this job, we could swim, eat good food, and party before going back to the unit. I also had a girlfriend and on at least one occasion had sex. This hotel had a lot of travelers coming through. I saw a Hampton's girls' sport team stay there for a few days. Many Nascar fans stayed there when events were going on.

To be honest, this was one of the best times of my life. It's at this place where I received my GED and saved money for my return to Grandy Park.

After about six months my time was up and it was time to take that ride to Norfolk, VA.

CHAPTER 5

I'M OUT

By the time I was released, my mom had moved from Grandy Park to Shoop Park. We now lived on St. Denis Ave. The difference between the two were one was in the projects and on St. Denis my mom was buying a house.

Fresh out with a fresh start one would assume that my chances at success are greater. However, what I found was that the man was out of the projects but the projects wasn't out of the man. I started hanging with some of the younger guys. All we did was party! Red Hot Chili Pepper was our spot. As a matter of fact, we used to call it going to work. I loved it when we met the girls from Bowling Park up there. Along with the partying, came a lot of beef. I was there when Lil "C" was shot. Needless to say, it wasn't long before I was hustling and then eventually getting high on the low. From there things went down pretty fast for me.

After being out for about 6 months, my younger brother was charged with shooting two guys at Tiny Giant off Lafayette Blvd. At the time, he was about 15 years old and was charged with first-degree murder and malicious wounding. I first saw it on the news then shortly he called me and I told him to come home. It wasn't too long later in the week the detectives came by and took him downtown. This was one of the hardest things I had to deal with up until this point because if I could, I would've taken those charges for him. It hurt me deeply to watch them take him away.

From that day until even now, my mother has never been the same. She began drinking uncontrollably until she lost her job, car, house and eventually her mind. She began to black out and walk the street night and day.

I was getting higher and higher. So, it wasn't long before I began robbing & stealing for my dope habit. One night I was on the prowl with my uncle trying to catch a victim and the police pulled me and found two guns in my car while I was already a convicted felon. To make a long story short, after about 30 days I went to court and took a plea deal to reduce it to a misdemeanor and time served. Can you believe they let your boy go while I was on parole and probation?

Upon my release going to see a P.O. was the farthest thing from my mind. So, in a matter of months I was back locked up for probation and parole violation.

Now I was back in 811 E City Hall waiting to go to court to find out my fate. During this time judges were giving out Detention and Diversion Center as an alternative to doing time so I asked for the programs and the judge approved.

The first part of this bid was the Detention Center on South Hampton. I knew plenty of guys up here too. Dukie, Rod and lots of guys were from the park. Also, one of the officers there was from Chesterfield Heights. The bad thing was that we used to give him a hard time in school and in their neighborhood. Dukie always reminded him that we did.

This place was like a military place with marching, canteen, and all the language we had to use. It was in this place where I began to read and really educate myself concerning life. I also learned a lot in our life skills class at this place that would come back to my remembrance when I finally was free from drugs and alcohol.

After my completion of this program I was shipped to the Diversion Center located in White Post, VA. Immediately upon approaching this building, you couldn't help but to notice that this is a prison. We were being stored in the Old Camp 7 building included with bars. Not only that but because this program is so new they didn't have any jobs set up for us yet. The Diversion Center was purposed to be a place to transition back in the community by working on the outside to gain experience and money to prepare you for your release.

However, for a couple of months we just sat and did nothing. It was during this time that I found out that my friend, Frashon was murdered. Fra, was one of the guys I knew my entire life. As a matter of fact, on this very bid he had come to see me a couple of times in 811. When I received the word that he had been killed it instantly made my heart heavy and burdened me. It also caused me to look over my life and examine myself and where I was headed.

After a couple of months, we moved next door to a warehouse style building without bars. I also gained employment at Melnor Inc., a lawn and garden production factory. On this job, I learned hand eye coordination and speed as the conveyor belts never stopped. I soon discovered that I really liked working because it gave me a sense of worth and satisfaction. While working, I befriended this guy from New Jersey named Dana.

Dana, was a Muslim guy who was working on his recovery from heroin. He had been all over the world scoring dope including Norfolk. As our friendship developed he asked if I want to move to the Winchester area to have a fresh start at life. After much talking and thinking I decided I would take that opportunity. Although I wasn't Muslim and believed in Jesus as Lord I decided to take a chance because he seemed to genuinely care about me.

After about six months, "I'm Out" again. I thought to myself, "Let's try this again." I wasn't ready last time, I just needed a do over, I thought.

Upon my release, I moved in with Dana in Winchester, VA—just as I said I would. I decided not to go home so I stayed in Winchester once I was released.

On that day, Anita came to pick me up from the center. After she picked me up she took me to the bank, shopping, and I believe to the liquor store. Anita was at my job and she offered to pick me up. She was married and we were only friends.

I soon began to work and after about a month a began to get home sick, I decided that I would take the Greyhound home to see my family and friends. Once I got to Norfolk my sister Trina and her boyfriend picked me up from the Greyhound Station. It didn't take long for me to find out that my momma had lost her house and was staying with my grandma Gloria. Not only did she lose the house, but she had put everything outside and people took whatever they wanted. So, I had no childhood pictures, no clothes, no trophy, or nothing that tied me to my youth.

Almost immediately I start doing dope again and it didn't take long to run through the couple thousand dollars I had saved. Next thing you know I got me a gun and was back to sticking people up again.

While I was locked up, I had met this guy name John. He was from P- Town and we had got out on the same day. We linked up and started a robbing spree on local dope dealers. The both of us together were HELL. This guy was down for whatever and I had plenty of heart. No good can come from us hanging out.

One morning I was awake by my Aunt Carolyn. She had heard about us on the streets. The word was that people were looking for me to kill me. My Aunt told me to call Dana to see if I could go back to Winchester. So, I called Dana and after convincing him that I was ready for change he agreed to allow me to come back.

That very day my Aunt drove me from Norfolk to Winchester. This was one of the longest rides I every took because I was dope sick and burning. Back in the WINC it's a slower, calmer living that will allow me to get back on my feet.

After going to the clinic and overcoming my cold turkey period I found a job and went to work. For the first time in my life while free, I began to hold down a job and learned to budget, plan, and set goals. About six months later, I heard that my sister Katrina was having problems in school and with my mother's husband, in which violence was a result of her actions so I went to Norfolk and my mom gave me guardianship of her. We got her back to Winchester and enrolled her in a GED program at Handley High School then later she went to Job Corps.

Not much later, I filed for custody of my son Bryon who lived in Norfolk with his mother. They weren't present at the hearing however, the judge gave me temporary custody of him. The problem was, I didn't know where they were. I went to the school where he should have been enrolled but he wasn't enrolled there nor did they live in the last known address that I knew.

I immediately took to the streets to ask questions and found someone who knew where they were. When the judge gave me custody, he told me if I found them to call the police and show them the paper that he had gave me. We found them in a hotel in Ocean View, the police knocked on the door and Bryon and his sister were in there. They brought Bryon out to me and I asked him are you ready to go with me and he said, "Yes." So, I told him to go get his clothes and anything that he wanted to bring. After he returned to the vehicle, I asked him was he surprised to see me and he responded by saying, "No, I knew you were going to come get me." At that response, I almost broke down in tears because it showed the faith of a child.

This was the beginning of the journey of myself, my sister, and my son in Winchester, VA. In this journey, it was our pain and experiences that kept us together. It was the rejection, neglect, and abandonment that caused us to believe in each other and to care for one another. It was the vision of our future that gave us the power to wake up, dress up, and show up. Times were difficult and we had to learn a new system or way of living. Outside of our comfort zone is where we lived. In this place, God preformed miracle after miracle— although at the time we didn't recognize them. It's looking back where we notice that it had to be God all along.

In this time, I'm drinking daily and my life is unmanageable although I'm working every day. The partying, lying and cheating is taking a hold of me. I'm tired and exhausted, depressed and hopeless.

CHAPTER 6

HELP ME

The first step in escaping a prison is to realize you are in one.I was imprisoned by my desire for drugs and alcohol. It forced me to devote much of my time and energy trying to fulfill it. These desires enslaved me for years and I had been crying out to no avail.

Finally, I have hit rock bottom and this life seems unbearable. I can't take another second, minute, nor hour in this state of mind.

Without thought right in my house while intoxicated, I began to call out to God. In that moment, I was ashamed and embarrassed because I had called out to God many times before to deliver me. God has delivered me on many occasions and each time He spared me, forgave me, delivered me, and I turned back when I promised Him I wouldn't. So, this time I couldn't find the words and perhaps He had heard it all before.

Then these words proceeded from the pit spirit, "Help Me!

I NEED HELP!" No long prayer, no elegant of speech or intellectual conversation just a desperate cry from a lost soul.

After that cry, I went to bed and didn't think the following day when I woke up things were different. I was walking to the front door and I heard audibly, "You're Free." I immediately looked around to see who said that but quickly I realized it was God himself declaring my freedom. It reminds me of a passage of scripture, Psalms 18:6

In my distress, I called upon the Lord, and cried to my God for help; He heard my voice out of His temple, and my cry for help before Him came into His ears.

He Heard My Cry!

I was excited and knew in my soul that I was free. I soon found out what God had spoken to me. He didn't speak to the people around me. With joy in my heart, I called my Dad to tell him all that happened and to my disappointment he laughed. That conversation taught me a lot and served notice that everyone won't believe that God speaks to you nor will they believe that God will or can use you.

CHAPTER 7

WHO ME?

It wasn't long before I heard the Lord speak to me again. I was half asleep and half awake and very clearly, I heard the Lord instruct me to go to the jail to fill out an application to volunteer for Bible Study.

I instantly responded, "Who Me God?" I have been convicted of multiple felonies and I'm pretty sure those folks won't allow me to go behind them walls. Needless to say, I acted on the Word of God and as a result I was approved to go in to help the guys out with their class Reformers Unanimous. It wasn't long before they asked me to speak and share my story. Once I did, many were saved. As a result of that, the word got back to the Chaplin and he offered me my own night. Shortly, after I began my own night the guy that I started off helping became my assistant. We went from a group of 12 to 40 plus men in our class. I had to move from the classroom to the gym. I believe because of the success the Chaplin offered me a second day which was on a Sunday and I agreed.

It was about 18 months since I have been doing this and

everything was going great, then I get another word from the Lord instructing me to start pastoring and once again my reply was, "Who Me?"

At that time, it appeared every time I settled in and got comfortable, God moved me. Although this was not my plan or anything I ever prayed for, I trusted the Lord concerning this.

One day I was looking in the newspaper and a non-denominational church had an opening for an Associate Pastor, so I contacted the person in charge and was offered the position. Certainly, I was moving from faith to faith and God would manifest Himself every time I was obedient. Things began to happen that I never dreamed of and really began to understand what Jesus meant when he said, "Not my will but thy will be done." You see, none of the plans were mine, I was walking in my pre-ordained steps.

It came a time when my church at the time purchased a building in Strasburg for four million dollars and as we were preparing to move God spoke again saying, "Ask to stay here to start a congregation," and just like in times past I said, "Who Me?" I asked my Pastor and of course he allowed me to because God had already prepared the way.

Grace and Mercy Ministries was birthed because of a seed God deposited within me. It's been four years now and it's in that time many souls have been saved, many have been baptized, many have been set free from the spirit of addiction, many have been delivered from generational curses, sexual perversions, molestation, rape and abuse.

Deliverance is the children bread and although I didn't know it when I first got started God truly used me to set the captives free. Along the way, there has been many who have questioned my calling and my intentions but because my heart is pure and I have remained authentic, God has defended me in every trial.

The Grace that has been allotted to my life is not of my own. It belongs to the Lord. God has done exceeding, abundantly, and above all that I can imagine. Who would have thought that He would love someone like me? Just to think that He thought I was worth saving.

As I write this, tears are welling up in my eyes. My joy is full and I'm sure that victory is mine.

To all who are castaways, misfits, black sheep, and forgotten ones God has a plan for you to be great. If you are saying, "Who Me?" you are right where God wants you.

Drug treatment clinic builds on relationships with clients

By CHRISTOPHER EARLEY
The Winchester Star

WINCHESTER — As the region continues to cope with an epidemic of opioid addiction and its ravaging effects, one local clinic is working diligently to make an impact on the lives of those struggling with substance abuse issues by addressing the underlying problems that may be fueling their need for drugs.

Northwestern Community Services' Amherst Clinic, located at 1014 Amherst St., opened its doors in late October, and with such a need for comprehensive treatment in the area, Regional Substance Abuse Coordinator Tim May said the flow of clients has been steadily increasing.

An arm of Northwestern Community Services — a nonprofit organization that receives state, local and federal funding to provide

MORE INFO...

CONTACTING NORTHWESTERN COMMUNITY SERVICES

■ **PHONE:** 540-667-8888
■ **ONLINE:** nwcsb.com

services to people with substance abuse issues, mental health disorders and intellectual disabilities — the clinic offers an array of services, including intensive outpatient programs (IOP) for people without insurance, with Medicaid and others referred by other community organizations.

The clinic also has been providing IOP treatment to several of Winchester's drug court participants, May explained.

"I think that what we're doing is

See Clinic, Page A10

SCOTT MASON/The Winchester Star

As a former addict, Northwestern Community Services' Amherst Clinic's Bryon Johnson has a special connection with clients.

SCOTT MASON/The Winchester Star

Bryon Johnson (left) and Tim May stand in one of the meeting rooms at Northwestern Community Services' Amherst Clinic.

Case Manager Amy Orndorff said along with those responsibilities, her job can sometimes include simply letting clients know that someone is on their side.

"You just let them know someone is there who will pick up the phone, listen and advocate for them," she said. "Like Tim [May] said, we don't judge them, we meet them where they're at."

And along with a dedicated staff of therapists, counselors and case managers, the clinic's special asset is peer support, or a peer recovery specialist.

Bryon's ability to empathize with clients often helps them open up and offers hope in their fight for sobriety, May and Cummings said.

"What Bryon provides is invaluable," Cummings said. "He's lived this."

Providing tangible proof that a person

can emerge from the throes of addiction to live a healthy, productive and meaningful life, Bryon often takes clients out to eat, on fishing trips or even on short walks in the park, in part to show them there is a world out there that doesn't require the use of substances to enjoy themselves.

The relationships Johnson has forged with clients, May explained, allow them to see the treatment process as one that is there to help them, not judge.

"I relive some of the experiences just to get back in there with them and show them a way out," Johnson said. "I let them know that there is a way out, you don't have die like this, you don't have to live like this."

— Contact Christopher Earley at cearley@winchesterstar.com

This is a Portion of my book that God is birthing in me. My prayer is that someone will be encouraged by this knowing that it doesn't matter how you start because with Jesus all things are possible. I would like you to know that your past may be setting you up for your future!

CHAPTER 8

MARKETPLACE MINISTRY

On October 1, 2016, I accepted a job as a Peer Recovery Specialist at Northwestern Community Service Board. I have had never heard of this term how it seemed to fit me, and it was an emerging best practice.

Immediately, I went to Roanoke, VA for a week to be trained in what was then 42 hours DBHDS training by Robin Hubert and Jeffrey Leonard.

On October 7, 2016, I received that certificate for completing that curriculum. While in the training, I was able to learn that "Peer Support" or non-clinical support was a shared responsibility and mutual agreement. It is a relationship built on shared experiences around emotional and psychological pain. This really resonated with me because I lived and experienced with drugs & alcohol. I encountered trauma upon trauma. In the Peer Support relationship, I had to cultivate relationships with friends, colleagues, and other persons who provided the common understanding. When issues and experiences are impacting recovery, actively engage in care and personal decisions that promote recovery, discovery, maintain hope, re-establish a positive identity, discover personal power, create a recovery environment, and overcome the impact of trauma. As you can tell, these are the tools I needed to continue to transition my life as well as to provide support and facilitate change for anyone who is seeking sustained deliverance.

This training also had a module on Recovery Language in which I totally loved because in all the mental health and substance use language it seemed stigmatizing, demoralizing and demeaning. I believe the power of death and life is in the power of the tongue and they that love it shall eat the fruit thereof.

In the recovery language module, it described this language to be strong, powerful and transformative. It gave an example of the power of words by using the childhood chant of, "Sticks and stones may break your bones but words will never harm me," and showed that it was more of a defensive statement than a statement of truth.

The truth is, words do hurt and harm. This was totally true in my life because it brought up the fact that my mom used to tell me how I'll never be nothing, how I'm just like my daddy and how she hated me for that and I become what she declared.

So, I felt that this module was one of the best for me in that I will be able to consider my word choices use first person language, utilize positive statements, and words with respectful language because language matters. Jesus said it this way, "It is the spirit that quickeneth; the flesh profiteth nothing: the words that I speak unto you, they are spirit, and they are life." This proves that words can be life giving and life producing.

One of the other modules that blessed me and changed my marriage was the communication skills module. It assisted me to acquire effective communication skills, understand how communication can build trust, and examine how choice of words, tone of voice, and attitude can affect communication. The active listening and effective listening improved my marriage by 70%, bless God.

On November 14, 2016, I received my certification for Peer Recovery Specialist from Virginia Certification Board. This accomplishment was big for me considering I never went to High School. I received my GED in prison and was never a finisher but God will complete the good work in which He begins. At this time in my life, God is using me majorly in my marketplace ministries and I had no idea what marketplace ministry was. Many times God has used me for a thing without the title. A prime example is when I had a voice in the legal system with our local Drug Court and I am providing support for their participants individually and in groups. This opportunity was so rewarding because it was reciprocal and benefitted me as much as the participants that I served.

On December 15, 2016, in Richmond, VA, I received a certificate for the "Peer Support Whole Health & Resiliency

Initiative" by Magellan and the ability to facilitate this training. This was a person centered planning process. The (PCP) process looked at current patterns, interests, and strengths in ten factors such as stress management, healthy eating, physical activity, restful sleep, service to others, support network, optimism based on positive expectations, cognitive skills to avoid negative thinking, spiritual beliefs and practices and a sense of meaning and purpose.

Then using this information, the PCP process will help an individual to prioritize and focus on a health or resiliency factor in which they will set a goal that meets the impact criteria once a goal is set. The PCP process will shift to guidelines for creativity, weekly action plans, and establishing a system of peer support. One of the other phases that's embedded in my head is "Catch It! Check It! Change It!" This has to do with negative thoughts and negative self-talk.

Catch It early on, this involves knowing you are moving from fact to story. Check it over against what is actually going on. Change it to more appropriately reflect reality. I enjoy whenever I facilitate this training because, "I love it when a plan comes together."

On April 26, 2017, in Charlottesville, Virginia, I received my "Peer Recovery Specialist Curriculum Training of Trainers" Certificate by the DBHDS Office of Recovery Services. This was and is HUGE. There are only 12 trainers in Virginia for this curriculum that were hand selected. To God be the glory, I believe this is apostolic in nature and God has mandated me for such a time as this. What this means that I have the ability, authority, and power to set up trainings in Virginia with a group of 12 people at a time and charge whatever fee I deem appropriate. Yes, DBHDS has deemed me a competent partner in Peer Support to change the world one person at a time with them backing me. Whenever I think about this, I think about the scripture that says, "I will send you on a mission to open their eyes, and to turn them from darkness to light, and from the power of Satan unto God, that they may receive forgiveness of sins, and inheritance among them which are sanctified by faith that is in me" (Acts 26:18).

This is one of the most noticeable favors that God has bestowed upon me. He has given me the power to get wealth. God truly breathed this thing in me and out of me and I don't believe he is done yet. In fact, He's just beginning to manifest the plans and purpose that he has for my life that includes hope and a future that was predetermined before I was in my mother's womb.

On May 12, 2017, I received my "Peer Recovery Specialists Supervisors Training" Certificate in Fairfax, Virginia by DBHDS. This training included a lot of core values, core emphasis, ethics, and boundaries and gave insight on how to supervise a Peer Recovery Specialist since it was now an evidence based practices and was added to the continuum of care for SUD & MH. This training gave me the ability to effective supervise (7) Peer Recovery Specialists with guidelines by DMAS.

Therefore, my marketplace ministry has exceeded anything that I could've thought or imagined. The scripture, "I came that you may have life and have it more abundantly" goes well meaning to me as God has blessed me within "Superabundance" (John 10:10, KJV).

Recently, someone asked me for my bio for a current project that I'm working on in my marketplace ministry and I would like to share with you what I wrote:

Bryon is a Certified Peer Recovery Specialist and Supervisor with Northwestern SUB/MH Peer Program. He has personal experience with drugs, alcohol, and is in long-term recovery. Bryon supervises Northwestern's ED Program, United Way Programs, and Community Programs. Bryon's trainings and certificates included Registered Peer Recovery Specialist, DBHDS Trainer of Trainers for Peer Recovery Specialists, Supervisors Training Certificate, ASAM Skill Building Training Certificate, Medically Assisted Recovery Support Training Certificate, MRT Certificate, Whole Health & Resiliency Facilitator, Mental Health First Aid Certificate, and he also leads Coffee & Kickin' It Peer Group.

I clearly remember the day I wrote that and in the moment I began to realize how far God had brought me and His faithfulness to an unworthy vessel. The one thing that sticks out to me is that I never chased any of those accolades. I only chased God and those are only some of the things that came as a result of me chasing Him.

CHAPTER 9

THE ROAD TO PASTOR BRYON

In this chapter I would like to take you on a journey to share with you how I became the Pastor and founder of Grace & Mercy Ministries.

I would like to start with the moment that I heard God announce that I was "Free." Shortly after that, I began volunteering at the jail leading Bible Study and sharing my story. While doing this for approximately 18 months beginning on February 1, 2012 and many souls were saved. It was here that I noticed that God had his hands on me and I was called to be the voice to a dying people.

On January 27, 2013, I had my initial sermon at Zion Baptist Church under the leadership of Rev. Delbert Hicks. I preached from Matthew, Chapter 1 on the genealogy of Jesus. I remember for weeks leading up to this day my anxiety was very high and it was difficult for me to sleep. I was nervous and I didn't want to mess this up although; I knew I was called by God for such a time as this. There were about 40 people in attendance and some of my family came to Berryville, Virginia from Norfolk, Virginia.

I believed I preached for about 20 minutes in which seemed like hours. Everyone was encouraging and very supportive. After preaching, Pastor Hicks along with all the other presbytery prayed, declared, decreed, announced, and commissioned over me. Minister Bryon was my title in and outside of Zion Baptist Church. Honestly, most people had a hard time seeing me as a minister because of my tattoos, gold tooth, and Timberland boots. While at Zion, I noticed that most of the ministers really weren't active in ministry in or outside the church. All of the ministers sat on the front row in service and only preached one time a year on a fifth Sunday.

My jail ministry was thriving and growing each week. I started out in a classroom with only a few guys and it didn't take long before the classroom became too small because of the amount of people that started to attend. It became a fire hazard with the amount of people we had so we started to host bible study in the gym each week. My mind was totally blown at what God was doing and at the fact that he was using me to do it. Next thing I knew, the Chaplin at the jail contacted me and ask if I could start a Sunday Service along with my weekly Bible Study and of course I jumped at the opportunity.

This didn't last but a few months before I realized I had took on too much. I worked 3rd shift at the time at a cookie factory and weekend work became the norm. At times I would get off at 6am, be at church at 11am, and then at the jail by 2pm, only to be back at work by 10pm. I was hungry for God and wanted to do the will of God. However, this proved to be too much so I asked Pastor John if he could take over the Sunday Service until I got off on weekends. He agreed that he would take it on. Now, all I had to do is run this by the Chaplin so I did and he was okay with it. I introduced them to one another and I was released from the Sunday Service at the jail while I continued Tuesday Bible Sunday.

Around April of 2013, while at home I was looking in the newspaper and saw that a church was looking for a Pastor. Something inside prompted me to call to set up an interview. I didn't think or feel that I was qualified but felt an overwhelming unction to make the call and to set up the interview. So, I made the call and Pastor Jay Ahlemann of Restoration Fellowship Church answered the phone. Needless to say we decided to meet fairly quickly at Perkins Restaurant one evening. I believe our meeting went extremely well and from the beginning you could tell that Pastor Jay had a way with words. On the streets, we call it the gift of gab. What I didn't know at the time was that Pastor Jay had previously filed bankruptcy because he was $4.7 million in debt when he was Senior Pastor of Church of the Valley. I don't know the details of this but evidentially there was a TV Station involved. What I did know was the same former Redskins players had attended and still attend his church.

I believe that Pastor Jay really hired me because I was black and he really wanted to reach other ethnic groups because his church was about 99% white.

On May 20, 2013, I was ordained as a Pastor of Restoration Fellowship Church. It was here that God began to teach me how to hear him with clarity without the music that I was used to, without the preaching that I was use to, and without the people I already knew. Everything around me was different and I totally felt out of place. God used this place so that I may know Him in a more intimate way. I learned to worship even when I didn't like the music and learned to hear him when I really didn't like the style of the preaching.

After a few months I realized that this was a very political church. It became clear why they were always saying they represented God and country. In June of 2013, Pastor Jay and Restoration Fellowship church bought back the church that they had once lost for the price of $4 million dollars. As they prepared to move to their new building, I asked Pastor Jay if I could stay in the current building to Pastor a congregation there. Pastor Jay said that I could and gave me his blessing to have an extension of Restoration Fellowship Church under my leadership. However, the owners of the building weren't too fond of a black man leading a congregation in the building that they had owned. After hearing this, I brought it to Pastor Jay's attention and Pastor Jay told me to ride around the building until the owner left the 8 o'clock service in which he continued to preach every Sunday.

On the first Sunday I was to start having, service was pretty intense because of the potential disruption from the owners who didn't want a black preacher there. Our first service did go well without any issues and the small crowd that we had really enjoyed themselves along with the food in the Middletown location.

After about six months or so, I discovered a few issues with our finances among other things so I asked Pastor Jay if we could start our own church, handle our finances, and pay rent for the building. He gave me his blessing.

Grace & Mercy Ministries

At the time, we had already applied to be a 501©3, secured the name Grace & Mercy Ministries, and had a board. Now we were actually becoming what God had showed me some years ago. Although it wasn't coming together in the way I thought it would, it was manifesting for sure.

In July of 2014, we acquired a building located at 5488 Main Street, Stephens City, Virginia. While baptizing about seven people in the river located in Strasburg, Virginia someone mentioned that this building would be becoming available. Our board discussed it and decided to rent the location when we only had about ten people at the time. We believed that if we changed the location to a more populated area more people would come and that's exactly what happened.

When we moved to this location we decided to join Bishop

Lyle Dukes of Woodbridge, Virginia Network so that we would have someone to not only cover us but to guide, correct, and encourage us. This network was and is a good group of people to belong to. Every third Monday we had a conference call whereby Bishop gave updates, encourage, imparted and declared the Word of the Lord for us along with casting vision. This was a great opportunity for me in which we attend the conferences, he laid hands on me and I was able to pray before thousands of people on a number of occasions. We had access to a plethora of material that would make it easier for our administration. During this time many people came to know Christ and were baptized. Some of the people that I met in my jail ministry started to attend our church. God made our church a safe place for people who had similar experiences as myself.

Very early on we began to get attention by the local newspaper. The first article about me and the church was titled "Thankful for Redemption." The article began like this, "A former heroin addict and prison inmate is celebrating his first anniversary as Pastor at a new church in the area, and he is calling on those who need help and those who want to help others to join him in ministry."

The article stated that we recently purchased a school bus that would help the Winchester Area Temporary Thermal Shelter (WATTS) for winter.

We would pick up the homeless from various points in Winchester and take them to participating WATTS churches every night for 13 weeks.

It included that we would also help with transitional housing for former inmates, and looking for ways to help stem the heroin problem in the area.

It also included how Governor Terry McAuliffe restored my rights in March. This was a personal victory.

On January 26, 2016, I had another personal victory. On that day I received my Bachelor of Ministry Degree from College of the Open Bible. This was a huge accomplishment for someone who hadn't complete 8th grade and acquired a GED while incarcerated.

Everything was going great and God was continuing to provide, protect, and fulfill every promise that He had said. On Friday July 15, 2016, tragedy came by way of fire. Around 5:30pm of that Friday, I received a call from the Fire Marshall indicating that the church had caught fire and I needed to come to the church. No one was at the church during the time that neighbor noticed the fire. By the time I got there, they had cut open the roof, put out the fire, and was trying to determine what was the cause of the fire. As I walked through the church, it was clear that it was significant damage, and it would be costly. The add on part where the kitchen was located looked totally destroyed. The sanctuary only appeared to have soot and smoke damage. At the time, we had a huge cross on the wall directly behind the pulpit that appeared to be totally unscathed by the fire. It was a picture of victory on the cross for me and a sign that God was still in control.

While trying to find a temporary place to worship, Pastor Jeff Beard offered his place on Kern Street located in the Northside of Winchester at 3pm. We began having service on Kern Street the following Sunday only missing one service by the grace of God. This was a very critical time for me as I had to remain in faith while our church home was destroyed. We had no idea if we would be returning. I believe this was a time that God was developing me and my level of commitment. As you know everyone was talking and asking questions about the fire. Some even thought that it was God's doing and that He was shutting our ungodly church down.

Exactly one year later a newspaper article was released with the headline, "Pastor sued after accidental fire at Stephens City's, Grace & Mercy." This article read like this, "A year after an accidental fire substantially damaged the Grace & Mercy Ministries Church, the pastor is being sued." Nationwide Insurance – A Fortune 500 Company that had nearly $210 billon in total assets last year, according to its annual report – wants the Rev. Bryon Johnson to repay the $148,000 it paid to cover damage from the fire that occurred July 15th of last year. The lawsuit, which also seeks legal costs, was filed July 11 in Frederick County Circuit Court.

The lawsuit said, "The fire caused extensive structural and smoke damage, throughout the building at 5488 Main Street, Stephens City, Virginia."

The approximately 40 member congregation returned to the church in December, according to the landlord and insurer Denise Medley. The fire was due to an unattended hot plate that someone forgot to unplug when they left the church, the lawsuit states.

Other than the accusation that Johnson violated the lease, it's unclear why Nationwide is suing the Pastor of a small-town church for an accidental fire.

As you can imagine everyone in town was whispering, talking, and gossiping concerning this article—But God.

This was certainly another tool that God allowed so that he could mature me and teach me that the Battle is the Lords.

During this time I believe a spirit of depression fell on me that nearly took a week for me to be delivered from. My eating habits, sleeping habits, and mental focus was impacted negatively by this experience greatly.

One day I decided to call in from work because of the heaviness and while at home God instructed me to put on some worship music on the TV in which I did. Within a matter of minutes, I went from listening to full blown worship to tears. I felt the spirit of heaviness released from me and I immediately felt lighter and had a sense of clarity. I called my wife who was at work to tell her what had happened and she was over joyed for me because she had a front row seat to witness what I was going through. Despite it all, I truly learned the faithfulness of God and how not to allow myself to be emotionally hijacked. By this time, our Ministry Grace & Mercy had overcome many obstacles that were sent by hell to literally kill us because of the souls that were being snatched out of hell. Our ministry had baptized at least 45 people, hundreds were led to Christ, and House of Grace Recovery House for men had been established all at the hand of God. As I look back now, it was what I would call a "Vision without a dollar" that was manifested by God himself through obedient vessels. One of the things I'm proud of besides feeding, clothing, and providing for the lost is our Annual Grace & Mercy Prom in which was started because many of us never attended our Prom due to various reasons.

In August of 2016, we attended a service in Harrisburg, Pennsylvania at St. Paul's Missionary Baptist Church where Apostle John Eckhardt was preaching and activating. I know some of you are thinking, "An Apostle at a Baptist Church?" However, I will have you know that this church operates in all the gifts of the spirits. They believe and utilize the five-fold ascension gifts and cast out devils.

It was here where I first encountered Apostle Melvin Thompson III who would soon be my Spiritual Father. That New Years of 2017, I decided to worship at Apostle Melvin's church All Nations Evangelistic Church in Harrisburg, Pennsylvania. It was here where I became familiar with the term Apostolic, Prophetic, and Deliverance. This one encounter at this church prompted me to join his network. I knew I needed what he had if I wanted to be successful in saving and transforming lives to the kind of people sent to our church. I knew that I would need training in Deliverance.

I knew that I would need to know how to pray governmental prayers. I knew I would need to know how to uproot, tear down, destroy, how to build, and how to plant.

In March of 2017, our church decided to ask Apostle Melvin if he would cover us, let us be a part of his network, and be my Spiritual Father. After a couple of calls, discussion, and paperwork we became a part of All Nations Apostolic Network.

This has proving to be one of the single greatest decisions that we have ever made to date. Being a part of this network, answered a lot of questions that I had from being in traditional denominational churches that lack the true power of God. I have now learned languages to what God has and is doing in my life. I'm now connected to a network that facilitates apostolic relationships with ministry leaders across ethnic denominational and cultural barriers. ANAN provides apostolic covering, accountability, and training for itinerant ministers, emerging leaders, market place ministries, senior leaders, and senior pastors. We have a passion to apostolically preach and teach God's kingdom agenda. We help leaders who are stuck in traditional church settings, equipping them to deal with struggles that accompany being pregnant with vision, yet handicapped by tradition.

As I begin to conclude this book, Romans 8:28 comes to mind, "And we know that all things work together for good to them that love God, to them who are the called according to his purpose."

What I have found is that believers can undergo tragic circumstances that are part of His loving design for our lives. From them, He brings good.

Tangible benefits and moral growth is our portion for those who love God and are called according to His purpose. I have determined it was for this reason I was born.

CHAPTER 10

INNER HEALING
AND DELIVERANCE

Without a doubt, inner healing and deliverance are two of the strongest needs that exist in the body of Christ. Many people are wounded, depressed, confused, addicted, fearful, sick, angry, or bitter, and are seeking help, to no avail. Because of this, I believe all churches need to teach on and to have ministries for inner healing and deliverance.

My own experience is that I was marvelously delivered from a spirit of fear that has so freed me that I want others to be freed as well. You cannot imagine how grateful I am that God freed me from this debilitating bondage that kept me from living an abundant life in Christ. My deliverance occurred the same night I received the baptism of the Holy Spirit. I knew something unusual had happened to me but was unsure of exactly what that was until later.

In 2004, I had several people prophesy to me that God would use me in the inner healing and deliverance ministry.

That year I also went through a program called the Elijah House Basic 1 School for Prayer Ministry (Elijah House, Post Falls, Idaho). This training was invaluable to me for my own inner healing and also for teaching me how to lead others through this process.

At the conclusion of our Elijah House training sessions, a man who attended the sessions addressed the class. This Christian man was also a psychiatrist, but only the instructor knew this information. In essence, the psychiatrist said that the field of psychiatry did not have nearly the success in healing people of their problems that the ministry of inner healing does. He gave God the glory as he heard and saw the benefits of the inner healing ministry. He gave the class his blessing and released us all to minister in this field. When he released us, I actually felt like I caught, or received something. I believe this is what we call an impartation. In October 2007, we officially launched the Inner Healing and Restoration Ministry in our church and have had very good results from this ministry.

Ministering in These Gifts

Inner healing is all about the cross and the resurrection of Jesus Christ. One of the first things we do when we minister to people is to determine their relationship to Jesus. If they don't have a relationship with Him, we ask if they would like one. It has to be about Him and what He has already done.

"The Spirit of the Lord is upon Me, because He has

anointed Me to preach the gospel to the poor; he has sent Me to heal the brokenhearted, to proclaim liberty to the captives and recovery of sight to the blind, to set at liberty those who are oppressed" (Luke 4:18).

When Jesus read the scripture from Isaiah 61:1-2, He said, "Today this scripture is fulfilled in your hearing" (Acts4:21). Jesus was letting the people know that HE was the one Isaiah prophesied about. He was announcing to them that The Holy Spirit had come upon Him to do these things. The people hearing this could then begin to understand that Jesus was the one that the Spirit of the Lord anointed and consecrated to preach, heal, set captives free, and open blind eyes. Jesus was affirming that this scripture was-and is-the essence of His ministry.

This ministry that Jesus began on earth has been delegated to His Church. By the capital-C Church, I mean the church of today, not just the early church. By Church, I mean us. We are the Church. YOU and I are the Church.

We have now been anointed to do the same things Jesus did, and even greater things, according to John 14:12. He told us to go and preach the gospel, heal the sick and cast out demons. Jesus said whatever we ask in His name, that He would do, so the Father is glorified (John 14:13). Every mighty act that is done in ministry is done in the name of Jesus. This is rightly so because He is doing the work through us. Remember that Jesus:

- Died so we might live.

- Bore our sins so we could be forgiven.

- Took stripes on His body so we could be healed.

- Became a curse for us so, we could be blessed.

Biblical Basics for Inner Healing and Restoration

The inner healing and deliverance ministries are all about Isaiah 61:1-3 and Luke 4:18. They are about what Jesus has already accomplished for us. They are about bringing wholeness to the people of God. They are about healing deep wounds. They are about restoration as Jesus restores our souls. They are about feeling loved and forgiven by Jesus.

The Bible gives us direction in this key ministry. We are to:

- Preach the gospel to the poor. We must proclaim the good news of what Jesus did for us to the poor in spirit, to the afflicted, to those who don't know about the atonement. The atonement includes more than salvation; it also includes healing and wholeness. "Surely, He has borne our griefs and carried our sorrows; yet we esteemed Him stricken, smitten by God, and afflicted. He was wounded for our transgressions, He was bruised for our iniquities; the chastisement of our peace was upon Him and by His stripes, we are healed." (Isaiah 53:4-5)

- Heal the brokenhearted. People who have been emotionally hurt by someone or who have had a loved one die whose wounds have not been healed have an

61

opportunity to be ministered to in inner healing. Psalm 147:3 says, "He heals the brokenhearted and binds up their wounds."

- Proclaim liberty to or set the captives free. Those in captivity cannot rescue themselves without some help or assistance. We need to teach that liberty and freedom are available to us. We need to know that the enemy can only hold us captive to sin if we give him the right to be there. Freedom comes when we repent and renounce sins of unforgiveness, bitterness, hatred, anger, etc. Galatians 5:1 says to, "Stand fast therefore in the liberty by which Christ has made us free, and do not be entangled again with a yoke of bondage."

- Opening of the prisons to those who are bound. There are a number of people who, even though they are saved, still feel bound or tied to old sins, bound by besetting sins, bound by inferiority, bound by rejection, bound by insecurity and unworthiness, or bound as a result of generational bondages, curses, or iniquities. Inner healing can help free God's people.

- Restore sight to the blind. This group consists of the deceived, those who don't know the truth or don't believe the truth. The truth will set us free, but we need to know it, believe it and practice it. The Word of God, spoken in love, can open spiritual eyes. His words are the key.

- Comfort those who mourn or are oppressed. People

who suffer from depression, or oppression, and those who are sad or heavily burdened can have these feelings lifted when the Spirit of the Lord descends on them. In inner healing, we anoint these believers with oil and pray over them, asking the Holy Spirit to come and saturate them with His presence.

Being wounded can cause us to be bitter and harbor unforgiveness; and while God understand our pain, He nevertheless wants us to know that unforgiveness is a sin and carries a penalty. Notice the language in the following scriptures:

"For if you forgive men their trespasses, your heavenly Father will also forgive you. But if you do not forgive men their trespasses, neither will your Father forgive your trespasses" (Matthew 6:14-15).

"And his master was angry, and delivered him to the torturers until he should pay all that was due to him. So my heavenly Father also will do to you if each of you, from his heart, does not forgive his brother his trespasses" (Matthew 18:34-35).

In an inner healing and restoration ministry session, we provided a safe setting whereby we can demonstrate the love of Jesus to the one looking to be healed. We allow the person seeking healing and restoration to discuss his or her wounded heart, hurt, and pain without any judgment or condemnation. With the help of the Holy Spirit, we seek to locate the root cause of the pain, and through confession, repentance and forgiveness prayers, the burden is lifted and the person is set free.

Inner healing and deliverance should be available to all who desire it. But we must desire it; we must want to be restored to wholeness. In John 5:1-9, there is an interesting story in this vein about a man who had an infirmity for 38 years.

This man way lying by the pool of Bethesda along with others who were sick, lame, blind and paralyzed. Many people went there because they believed that if they got in at the right moment, they would be healed. When Jesus saw this particular man and knew he had been in that condition a long time, He asked the man, "Wilt thou be made whole?" (John 5:6, KJV). We too must ask ourselves whether we really do want to be made whole. This man gave Jesus some excuse about not having anyone to put him in the water before someone else gets in it. How many of us know that this is not a good response when Jesus asks you if you want to be made whole? The obvious response is, "Yes, Lord!"

I believe this man was in that condition so long that he lost sight of why he was there. His belief system was that if he were the first one in the water, it would heal him. That was as far as he could believe.

People spend lots of money on medication, secular therapy, and counseling, and that may be necessary and good for them. But, I know a man who said He came to set captives free, and to heal broken hearts. His name is Jesus. Have you tried Him?

If we:

- Are struggling with something, Jesus can help us; seek His help.

- Are in bondage, Jesus can free us.

- Have deep wounds, Jesus can heal us.

- Are under a generational curse, Jesus can break it.

- Suffer from rejection or abandonment, Jesus is there to love us.

- Are oppressed or depressed, Jesus can deliver us.

- Have a heavy burden or spirit of heaviness, Jesus can lift it.

- Are blinded to the truth of God's Word, Jesus can open our eyes.

The Great Exchange

The good news is when we offer our brokenness to God, He is ready and waiting to exchange it for something significantly better-wholeness. The Scriptures tell us about three changes in particular that relate to inner healing and deliverance. God is waiting to give us:

- Beauty for Ashes. We will rise out of the ashes of abuse, of unworthiness, and of shame from being a victim. We will become victorious. We will come to know who we are in Christ. We will come to know we

65

are secure in Him. We are loved by Him.

- The Oil of Joy for Mourning. Sadness, gloom, and depression will be replaced with joy. When we learn that the joy of the Lord is our strength, it will lift our spirits. When we receive the truth of God's Word for us, it will bring joy to our hearts. Our mourning will be turned to dancing (see Psalm 30:11).

- The Garment of Praise for the Spirit of Heaviness. Our burdens will be lifted. Guilt will go, and shame will disappear. We will now be able to praise the one who set us free. His name is Jesus.

Be Loosed from Infirmity

A number of people who suffer from chronic physical illness are really bound or affected by a demonic spirit. In Luke 13:10-16, we have an account of Jesus teaching in a synagogue on a Sabbath. While teaching, He noticed a woman who had a spirit of infirmity for eighteen years. She was bent over and could not straighten herself up. (This would be someone we would describe as having something like scoliosis, or kyphosis of the spine, or some type of arthritis.) In verse 12, Jesus spoke and said, "Woman, you are loosed from your infirmity." When Jesus laid His hands on her, she was made straight. When the religious leaders questioned Jesus about healing this woman on the Sabbath day, Jesus responded to them, "So ought not this woman, being the daughter of Abraham, who Satan has bound for eighteen years, be loosed from his bond on the Sabbath?" (verse 16).

The woman in this example was freed from a spirit of infirmity that had bound her for a long time. This tells us that some of the sicknesses we have in our bodies are rooted in various demonic spirits who have taken up residence in us. When we are freed or delivered from a demon spirit, often times we will experience improved physical health.

I know that for me, the spirit of fear that had me in bondage for most of my life was debilitating. It kept me from doing some things that I would have liked to do, as well as keeping me from being all that I could be in the body of Christ. This fear had power over me. This fear put limitations on me. This fear brought anxiety and worry. But thanks to God, I was delivered from this spirit in 1997, and interestingly enough my health also improved.

As believers, we can expect that God can, and will, release us from the influence of demonic spirits. Whatever we're dealing with, whether it is fear, rejection, lack of trust, mental torment, feeling unworthy, or being victimized by abuse or neglect, nothing is too difficult for our Savior to heal and deliver us from.

Inner Healing is for Today

There are a number of persons suffering from a variety of issues such as fear, anger, rejection, abandonment, gender identification, generational curses, addictions, etc. They are saved individuals but are struggling to hold on and live a victorious life in Christ. This group could benefit from inner healing of wounds through prayer ministry.

This is why inner healing and deliverance are for the Church today. If a local church needs training in this area, it should find someone who specializes in this ministry, and who could come in and begin to train and equip the body. Such a church will be much healthier and stronger. This is what we did in our local church, which was a traditional Baptist church. We sought out and brought in people who could help us become equipped in various areas of ministries.

We had someone come in who introduced us to, and taught on, deliverance. This included generational curses, demonic entry point, and the authority of the believer. We later advanced to how to pray for physical healing and for those needing inner healing and deliverance.

Our people were also encouraged to attend seminars and conferences where they could not only learn about, but receive prayer and impartation from the person with the anointing and gifting. We now have saints who know their spiritual gifts and minister to others as the Holy Spirit leads them. They can also now teach and minister in these matters.

As believers, we have the authority from Jesus and the power from the Holy Spirit to represent Jesus on earth. He said, "And these signs will follow those who believe: In my name they will cast out demons…" (Mark 16:17). We can pray that God will give us a burden for setting people free through our prayers. We are the hands, feet, and mouth of Jesus on earth. We need to use them for the glory of God.

Speaking Inner Healing Words Based on Scripture

I dwell in the secret place of the Most High and I abide under the shadow of the Almighty. Psalm 91:1

The Lord will give His angels charge over me, to keep me in all my ways. Psalm 91:11

He who is in me is greater than he who is in the world. 1 John 4:4

I sought the Lord and He heard me, and delivered me from all my fears. Psalm 34:4

Many are the afflictions of the righteous, but the Lord will deliver me out of them all. Psalm 34:19

God did not give me a spirit of fear, but of power and of love and of a sound mind. 2 Timothy 1:7

No weapon formed against me shall prosper, and any tongue that rises against me in judgment shall be condemned. Isaiah 54:17

I will not be afraid of sudden terror, nor of trouble from the wicked when it comes, for the Lord will be my confidence. Proverbs 3:25-26

The Lord is my light and my salvation; whom shall I fear? The Lord is the strength of my life; of whom shall I be afraid? Psalm 27:1

For in the time of trouble God will hide me in His pavilion;

In the secret place of His tabernacle He will hide me. Psalm 27:5

Even though I walk through the valley of the shadow of death, I will fear no evil; for the Lord is with me; His rod and staff are a comfort to me. Psalm 23:4

I will not be afraid of the terror by night, nor of the arrow that flies by day. Psalm 91:5

I will not let my heart be troubled, neither will I be afraid. John 14:27

God will heal my broken heart and bind up my wounds. Psalm 147:3

I will cast my burden on the Lord and He will sustain me. Psalm 55:22

I will be anxious for nothing, but in everything by prayer and supplication, with thanksgiving, I will let my requests be made know to God. Philippians 4:6

The peace of God which surpasses all understanding will guard my heart and mind through Christ Jesus. Philippians 4:7

If I forgive men their trespasses, my heavenly Father will also forgive me; but if I do not forgive men their trespasses, neither will my Father forgive my trespasses. Matthew 6:14-15

I must bear with, and forgive others, and if I have a complaint against someone; even as Christ forgave me, so I also must do. Colossians 3:13

I will not let bitterness, wrath, anger, clamor, evil speaking and malice abide in me. I will be kind to others, tenderhearted, forgiving others, even as God in Christ forgave me. Ephesians 4:31-32

Prayer

Lord God, I pray that your will and purpose for my life be fulfilled in the manner in which you planned it. I repent of every wrong and ungodly desire, attitude, behavior, and pattern of thinking. Forgive me for holding on to these behaviors and habits. I renounce and reject them. I am standing on the truth of our Word, which says whatever I bind and loose on earth has been bound and loosed in heaven. In the name of Jesus, I break the power and effect of harsh words or curses spoken about me, to me, or by me. I break generational curses and all sicknesses that have occurred in my family. They have no more effect upon me or any member of my family. I speak these words in the name of Jesus Christ, who has given me the keys and authority to do so. Amen.

(This chapter contains an excerpt from Pastor Audrey C. Jackson's book, "The Church – Functioning in Miracles, Signs, and Wonders." Used by permission. This book can be found on Amazon.com, and Water-rock.com. Audrey Jackson is a teacher of the Bible who has had a hunger and thirst for God's Word since the day she was saved and has been a mentor to me and my family.)